Original title:
"The Lionhearted Spirit"
Copyright © 2023 Loomevalgus OÜ
All rights reserved.
ISBN 978-9916-725-04-7

It is only through labor and painful effort, by grim energy and resolute courage, that we move on to better things...
Theodore Roosevelt

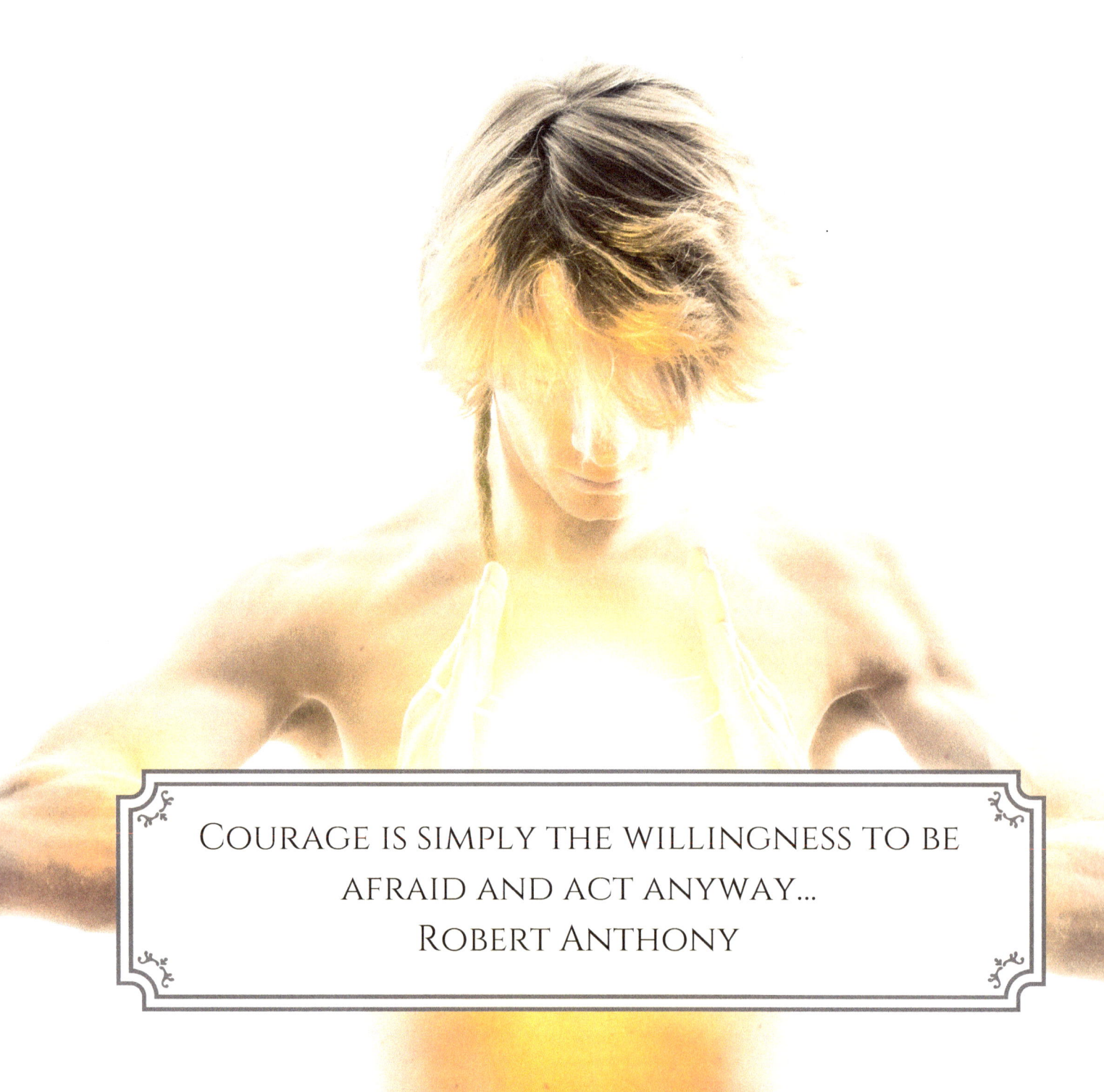

Courage is not the absence of fear, but rather the judgement that something else is more important than fear...
Ambrose Redmoon

Success is not final, failure is not fatal: it is the courage to continue that counts...
Winston Churchill

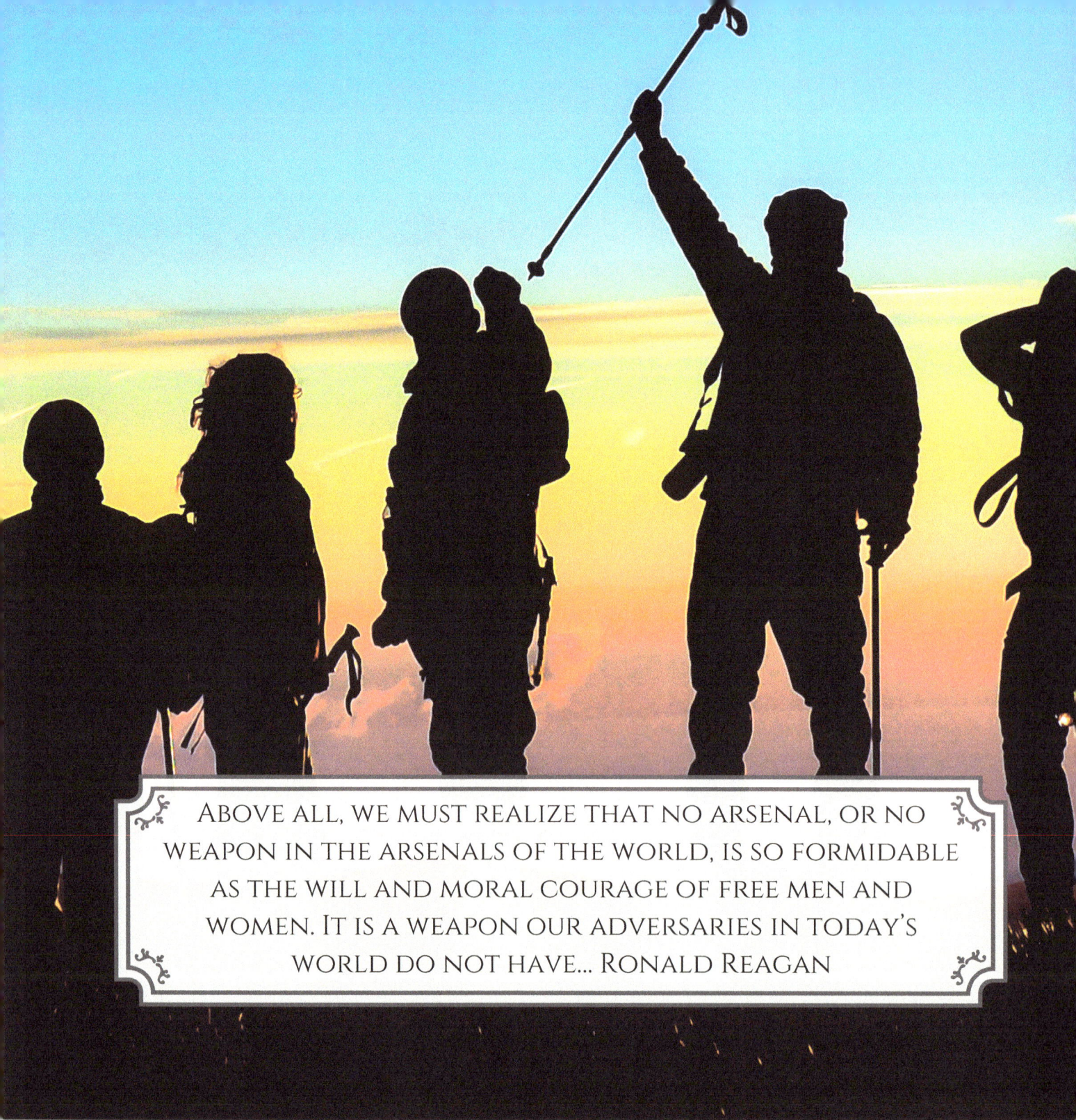

A LOT OF PEOPLE DO NOT MUSTER THE COURAGE TO LIVE THEIR DREAMS BECAUSE THEY ARE AFRAID TO DIE...
LES BROWN

> I AM NOT DISCOURAGED, BECAUSE EVERY WRONG ATTEMPT DISCARDED IS ANOTHER STEP FORWARD...
> THOMAS A. EDISON

Ingram Content Group UK Ltd.
Milton Keynes UK
UKHW050208140423
420118UK00003B/44